my bleeding heart

makenzie labani

to the readers, who give me
the chance to live my dream, and
sticking by my side when everyone
else took a turn.

i thought you loved me,

but perhaps you didn't, perhaps

you loved the idea of me, and yet

i still write endless words

for you.

table of contents

heartache 7

heartbreak 71

author's note 115

the author 119

HEARTACHE

NONE OF IT MAKES SENSE

it all makes no sense.

how someone like him could be entangled in my love makes no sense.

the way he kisses me softly and tells me that he loves me makes no sense.

i'm a broken girl, unworthy of love

it makes no sense for him to want to be my whole world.

i deserve hatred, unfairness and doubt,

but he grabbed my arms and started shouting aloud,

im hers

it makes no sense.

the way he apologizes first after i punch him with my words makes no sense.

the way he forgives and forgets like i didn't do horrible shit makes no sense.

so, riddle me this:

how i'm damaged and broken beyond repair,
but you still love me and run your fingers
through my hair.

make that make sense.

SOMEONE WHO LOVES ME

i've made so many efforts to be perfect

i've done so many things to change myself to be perfect

i wanted to be liked, to be loved.

but i found someone that makes me feel

like everyone's around me and adoring me

i found someone who's convinced me that i'm pretty the way i am.

i found someone who tells me i'm perfect every morning to make sure i never doubt it.

i found someone who loves me unconditionally.

that person is you.

POWER

words are so powerful.

actions are so powerful.

feelings are so powerful.

but there's something more powerful than anything,

more powerful than power itself,

and that's

my love for you.

FOR YEARS,

for years, i thought happiness just wasn't meant for me.

for years, i thought that being loved, wasn't allowed for me.

for years, i thought i wasn't good enough

a useless tool unable to be amended to repair.

for years, i thought i was just a girl,

a damaged,

broken girl.

i was a porcelain doll with cracks along her face,

the bits of glass falling off with every heartbreak.

for years, i thought i was too hard to love.

for years, i thought i was too ugly to be pretty.

for years, i was never

happy.

but for a year, i finally think i can be loved.

for a year,

i think i am the prettiest girl,

who's scars and cracks can be kissed

instead of skimmed.

HATE OF LOVE

being loved and lost,

and i'm lost in this love,

a pain so powerful to shake,

but a happiness no one can break,

i hate you; i love you

i want you out of my life,

but i want you at my bedside,

i hate every minute i'm not with you,

but i love every second that you're gone,

you're annoying

but you're amazing

you're crazy

i'm crazy about you.

because loving isn't cherishing every word they say,

or admiring every day,

because perfect doesn't exist,

relationships are rocky and some beyond repair

but the love will always be there.

and i love you, but at the same time,

i also hate you.

PRETENDING

i try to not think of you

but you occupy every second of my mind

i gaslight myself—make me believe a lie,

tell myself the pile of pillows

and blankets is your arms.

i pretend a lot,

i pretend like i'm okay when

i want to scream out your name,

shout, cry, and weep till my voice runs dry.

i want you in my presence,

i want you near me laying

in my arms.

i see you when i close my eyes,

i pretend i see you in the halls passing by,

loving you is like breathing,

such a complicated process

yet so easy to do.

loving you is the only thing i know how to do right,

so i pretend i see you every night.

WONDERING WANDERERS

i wonder everything that can be wondered.

i wonder how the stars are so beautiful,

i wonder how the world works,

i wonder many things.

i wonder how someone could love me.

i wonder how people can leave, but he won't.

i wonder how someone like him likes someone like me.

i wonder how i

am his everything.

WHEN THE IMPOSSIBLE IS POSSIBLE

be my love forever until the end of time.

be mine until daylight doesn't come.

be with me until a pig learns to fly.

be mine forever,

and die with me in the grave.

YOU

i'm in love with you.

and there's simply no more to say.

DREAMS V. NIGHTMARES

if i could wish for anything in the world,
i'd say *nothing*.
i wouldn't wish for a thing because the wish
i made every birthday,
every night before bed,
the wish i made while i crossed my fingers
and repeated it in my head
came true.

the thing i always yearned for,
a boy who loved me,
came forth in my life so quickly
that i could barely even proceed to speak.
i was speechless in his presence,
lost in the caverns of his eyes.
staring at him blankly as he waits for a reply,
i'm a dreamer,

i've been a dreamer since 2009,

but i became doubtful of my wishes as

everything went to hell

but then he arose in the midst of the darkness,

turned what i thought was hell,

into a beauty of angels with love so swell.

EXPRESSIONS

love is expressed through so many things,
songs, poems, hugs or a simple kiss on the cheek
love can be seen everywhere,
in movies, words, schools, the world.

love is home, happiness, joy and cheer
yet it's sadness, harm, worry and fear
it's so many things,
in so many things,
expressed by so many things,

and yet i still can't figure out the right way to say
i love you.

PRAYERS

i preach but i don't pray,

god isn't in my favor,

i don't believe in angels,

but i believe you fell from heaven.

i call but i don't pray,

jesus isn't in my name,

i don't believe in heaven,

but i believe you're an angel.

i've never believed in anything,

religion, ghosts, true love, fantasy stories,

but i believe you're the one for me,

even if that's considered controversy.

ROMEO'S LOVE

you know i'm utterly obsessed with you, right?
are you aware that everything you do has me
locked in a chokehold?
growing up, i wished for a certain love,
Romeos kind of love
my other half, the final piece
to my wretched puzzle,
the kind of love that had me waking up,
admiring the birds chirping and thinking of you,
the kind of love that was, oh, so sweet and no
one even knew,

it wasn't secret but no one knew we kissed under
the stars that night,
it wasn't hidden but no one knew we said
i love you a thousand times that night.
i wouldn't hide you, i wouldn't hide your sweet,

effortless love

but no one will know what it's like to have an

angel in their

arms.

i'm not selfish—really, i'm not,

but you're mine regardless of what

fate or the distance says.

i'd give up everything, my soul, my heart,

everything i cherish because i cherish you

like Romeo does his juliet,

you're the kind of love i dreamt of,

the kind of love that leaves me

dumbstruck with every touch,

the kind of love that has me kicking my feet

with every enduring message i receive,

your kind of love.

and even though we both might die in the end it

won't matter as long as i'm still

holding your hand,

thus a kiss, thus i die, thus a love

once in a lifetime

and when you're in the distance and the reach is

all too far i'll bellow

where art thou romeo?

in my dreams there you are and

I've memorized every look you make

and that forsaken face,

and i remember that night.

the night of i love you, the night of the kiss,

the night that felt like nothing but bliss.

i hear *Romeo*, i hear *juliet*,

i hear *star crossed lovers* and there you are,

so far away and i can't meet your lips and

i've bellowed so long

where art thou Romeo?

my bellows turn into screams and

my screams turn into cries

but my Romeo will return and we'll start

a new playwright,

where the lovers don't die in the end.

Romeo and juliet take two;

the one with me and you.

LOVE NOTE

love.

love is to hold on to something you're afraid of losing,

love is to keep them in your heart even when your heart begins to break.

love is something that can't be beaten.

something that can't be changed.

something that gets back up when it's pulled down.

nothing could change the power of love,

nothing could change our connection,

because when love is true,

it's the most powerful thing to ever exist.

and our love.

it's almost more powerful.

MINE FOREVER

you've been mine forever,

since 2009—you've been mine.

you've been in the back of my mind, my prince charming, my soulmate, my one true love.
you've always been there, waiting for me to find you.

i saw you, and i knew.

i knew i had

recognized you;

my heart skipped a beat when i heard you speak and that's when i realized.

i had found *you*.

i had found the boy i longed for all those years.

all those years in sorrow, and wonder.

but there you were,

standing right in front of me, arms reach.

you are breathing, talking. you were alive.

the guy i thought only existed in my mind

was in love with me,

when i thought he didn't exist.

WORDS

i'm so in love with you,

and no one even knows how in love with you

i am;

not even you.

i've tried to explain but always seem to fail.

i've wanted to make people understand,

make you understand,

but it's much harder than that.

it's not as easy as saying *1, 2, 3*.

easier said than done, but not in this scenario.

i've never struggled with words,

i've struggled with math, science,

socializing and much more.

but, never words.

i've finally encountered a topic that stumps me—something i can't validate in words.

words that can't be validated.

the simple yet complex way,

that i'm in love with you.

THE CURE

i believe love has the power to cure all illnesses.

i believe love has the power to make someone think they're useful and they're everything.

i believe in this so strongly because it happened to me.

i hated myself. i hated the world and everyone in it.

i wanted the world to end so much

that i'd end my own world.

but he stopped me.

he cured me of the deadly illness of suicidal thoughts,

and everything became clear

once again.

TOGETHER

all the happiness in the world could not compare to how i feel around you.

next to you, the world seems to uplift, like a breeze on a magic carpet ride

next to you, the voice in my head turns down,

a soft ballad playing in the background.

with you, everything loses its weight.

with you, the heaviness on my shoulders falls off.

with you, happiness is the easiest thing to produce.

NEED YOU

wanting someone is liking who you are with them.

needing someone is being who you are with them.

i would sacrifice so much to be with you:

my dreams, my happiness.

but really, i'd be giving up nothing because

you're my dream, and you're my happiness.

helping someone is being a part of their journey.

saving someone is being the reason for their journey.

and you saved me, in every way i didn't know was possible.

in ways i had no idea people were capable of.

FIREFLIES

your smile,

your laugh,

the time you held my head against your chest when i said i felt sad—

that's when i realized i had fallen in love

fallen in love with a guy from the other side,

a guy i shouldn't be with but that soon passed my mind.

i needed you like nobody else,

you were the sunlight to my moonlight,

you were like fireflies in the sky that i dreamed of catching,

but the only difference is,

is that dream came true.

i caught you in my heart.

and when i was falling you caught me in your arms.

you said it's okay, it'll be fine

and i believed you.

and i loved you.

and to this day, i still love you.

because i caught you when you were flying,

and you caught me when i no longer could fly.

FALL

i've fallen in love with a guy.

this guy, when i see him, i lose all control.

i've fallen in love so deeply, that i couldn't even stop loving if i wanted to.

and believe me, i've wanted to.

because love is painful, scary, but so amazing, and sometimes you don't even want it.

falling in love young, as an expat, it's dangerous.

but i did, and there's no going back.

and every day, i fall even more.

because i've fallen in love with a guy.

who loves me

and cared,

and i just keep falling.

INVISIBLE STRING

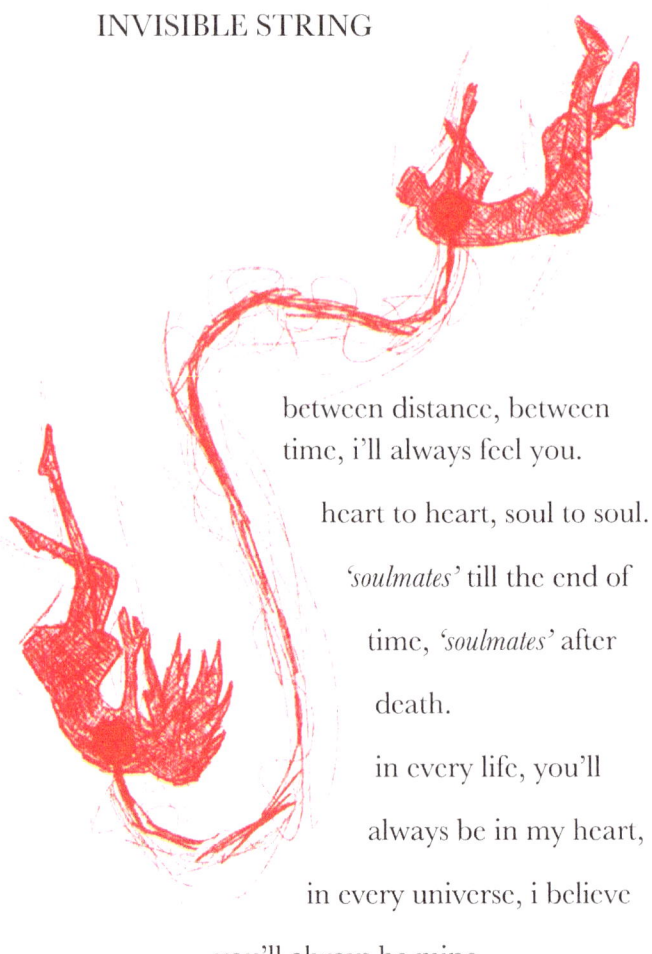

between distance, between
time, i'll always feel you.
>heart to heart, soul to soul.
>>*'soulmates'* till the end of
>>>time, *'soulmates'* after
>>>death.
>>in every life, you'll
>>always be in my heart,
>in every universe, i believe
you'll always be mine.
heart to heart, soul to soul. always connected
by some *invisible string*

UNANSWERED QUESTIONS

sometimes i wonder what life would be like if i hadn't met you.

if i hadn't met certain people.

if my life had been any different, who would i be?

would i still be *me*?

or would i be someone else?

there are so many things in life that contribute to our outcomes:

the people we meet, the deeds we do, the things we create.

there's an infinite number of questions

that can be asked and an

infinite number of answers.

however, some questions are left

unanswered.

i have a question that is yet to be answered,

an answer i've been seeking for a long time

but no one can say it right,

no can embed it in my head,

no one has explain,

written,

answered,

said,

good enough to make me believe

it's not a lie:

how does one love a person so damaged?

COLORS

roses are red,

violets are blue,

when i'm with you,

i see true color once again.

grass is green,

clouds are white,

i realize now what real life looks like.

i was living in black and white,

unaware of the beauty of the real world,

i refused color, because once you see

black and white feel so more dull,

but colors are made with black and white,

i was just blind to real life

roses are red,

violets are blue,

sunflowers are yellow,

and everything seems so adieu,

i realize

now,

how beautiful it is to accept that

colors mean happiness,

darkness means sadness,

but together they mean humane.

but we always say,

roses are red,

and violets are blue.

SOULS

i'd surrender everything, barter my soul and life

if it meant being with you.

ENOUGH

even though i ended up

depressed, unhappy and sad,

i still met you.

although i tried to kill myself one too many times

you showed up between it all

and convinced me everything'll be fine.

so maybe i'm weird.

maybe i am the bitch everyone says i am.

but i have you and they don't.

so, they can hate me,

judge me,

mock me all they want

but i have you and that'll

always be

enough.

CUPID'S SCARS

all the love in the world could not compare to the love of thee.

the stinging arrow of cupid left a scar on my back,

that had me talking nonsense of his eyes.

happiness, heart, loveth, and despair.

hold my hands and cover thyself in my love,

leave nothing but a drop,

for me to come back and dream for eternity and on.

HOME

where's home? they asked

home is in his arms—not a house nor a place.

home is nothing but his face.

home is the look in his eyes staring into mine.

home is him.

home is the love of my life,

the one that allows me to adore

the peace of time.

THAT MOMENT

i knew i was in love with you at that moment.

it wasn't the kiss, it wasn't the hug, it wasn't the *i love you* over and over again.

it was that one moment.

that quick flash of a second.

that moment when our eyes both met at the same time.

that moment when our pupils dilated to the same size.

that small glimpse of a memory,

the feeling when the world goes still,

and life seems like nothing else but the two of us standing there.

and then,

in that moment,

i knew that i loved you.

THE MEANING OF LOVE?

loving is so easy when *loving* means loving you.

PROTECTED HEART

i'll hold your heart together in my hands.

protect it from the good and bad,

keep it in my grasp.

i'll hold your heart so you can

forget the heartbreak,

and all things you've lost.

allow your heart to pulsate

within the warmth of my palms.

give me your heart,

let me love and cherish the

sweet

delicacy.

let me

love

you.

SWIM, BIKE, RUN

to keep above the surface,

you must swim,

to breathe,

you must live

if you stop pedaling a bike,

you fall over,

if you fall for him,

you forget how to pedal

a paralyzing emotion,

a world-pausing feeling,

a life-changing event,

you can run, but you cannot hide,

when i meet his eyes

i lose my mind,

i cannot suppress, i cannot push down

the feeling that i'm in love

and the feeling that i've met the one.

WITH YOU

happiness, love and joy

are the whole world,

the dream life everyone wants,

it means so much.

happiness, love, joy and peace

matter more than anything,

but it means nothing when it's not with you.

FEELINGS

being loved by you is like being loved by
an angel itself.
i don't believe in things like that
but if they were real,
i believe you are one.
i believe as though you were created in a lab,
curated perfectly for me.
maybe not perfect for everyone,
but my knight in shining armour.
i don't believe in heaven or hell,
i don't believe in angels and devils,
i don't believe in gods.
but i believe that you're a gift,
a blessing, something that was sent to earth
for me.
maybe that's selfish,
maybe that's inconsiderate,

or perhaps it makes zero sense.

most feelings don't make sense.

HOW I LOVE YOU

why can't you love me

you said to me once.

my bandaged heart started to break,

the stitches pulling apart,

beginning to disintegrate.

why can't you love me

and oh, god how wrong you were,

to say i didn't love you,

or to say you loved me more.

why can't you love me

with my whole heart and soul i love every

bit of you,

every part that cries and aches,

all the sides of you that shout and scream,

the ones that smile,

the ones that gleem.

why can't you love me

when the sun and moon align,

and the stars light up the sky

i'll kiss you softly—gently.

why can't you love me like i love you,

because i don't just love you like you love me—

i love you in silence,

and in spaces between

my love stretches further

than words know how to go.

i don't love you like you love me,

because i love you much more,

and i see you

in a way you could never see me.

UNDERSTAND

it's not easy to recognize,

but it isn't hard either,

it's not rocket science,

but you may still struggle to understand

why someone like him

loves someone like me.

i'm not a queen upon a throne,

someone worthy enough of him,

yet he still lays me on a pedestal

and tells me *i'm his.*

i've been broken so many times,

and robbed of true love,

but he still hugs me, and holds me, and tells me he's sorry

he fixed a heart he didn't break

yet he still feels guilty,

and i will always

struggle to understand

why any of that

makes sense

I WAS WRONG

i've wished for so long,

i've dreamt of everything,

to see santa and his reindeer,

but instead,

i saw you.

i thought love would be hard,

scary, rough,

an abomination—

a disgrace to society,

but it's not.

it's something so powerful

and incredible,

you realize how amazing the world truly is.

my wishes never came true,

but they brought along you.

THROUGH EVERYTHING

through it all,

through all the years,

the days,

the times i never felt okay

you stayed,

and loved me,

cherished me like everyone else,

didn't make me feel unworthy for being

who i was

you didn't leave,

you didn't run away,

you stayed by my side even when i shut you out

and through it all,

i always loved you.

YOU

every day when i see you,

my day gets a little brighter.

when i wake up,

i think of you the second the light

shines through.

you occupy my mind 99% of the time,

i couldn't even pretend,

lie,

forget or say goodbye

because the moment i see you in my eyes,

i realize how special it is

that you're

mine.

I'VE FALLEN IN LOVE

i think i've fallen in love with him.
i've fallen in love with someone i shouldn't have;
my ex's best friend.

but how could i not?
i catch his eyes in every class we share,
and i forget who i am.
he looks at me in a way that makes me feel seen.
when he looks at me, with his eyes soft,
it's almost as if i can hear him saying,
you're so pretty

i may be going crazy.
but i'm in love with him.
i'm so in love with him and i know i shouldn't be.
but it's far too late now.
i've fallen down a hole no one can get me out of,

not even him.

he could tear me to shreds,
use me like a worthless ragdoll,
and i'd still love him.
i'd let him take me over because
i love him.

you don't even know what love is,
my mom would say but what did i care?
i knew how i felt,
i was looking at a boy and
every part of me was screaming and
i was beginning to lose sight of reality.

i bring him up in every conversation because
my mind can't manage to think of anything else.
is this what love felt like?
this.

this is love.

i love you. i'd say, expecting the hurtful rejection.

i love you, too.

and then i knew,

i knew for sure,

just how in love i had fallen

LOVE IN THE SHADOWS

i hid you behind a wall,

loved you in the shadows,

kissed you in the dark,

where no one ever wanders.

i love you i said,

and i meant it

in the shadows.

behind a tree,

under the rain,

guarded by a lie,

and pressing your body against mine.

i love you i said,

and i meant it

in the shadows.

a small secret,

a little white lie,

a fairy tale and a fib,

the girl that cried *we're just friends*.

i love you i said,

and i meant it

even then

in the shadows.

i don't just love you with my heart,

i love you with my soul,

my body,

my mind.

i love you with every part of me.

every part of me that sweats,

and cries,

every part that aches

when you're away from my gaze.

i love you with every bit of me.

a desperate desire to find

peace amidst your chaos

and hold you 'till the sun grows cold.

i love you,

and i mean it now,

as we walk out of the shadows

and in to the light, where their

stares lie upon us.

HEARTBREAK

MY BLEEDING HEART

my heart bleeds far too easily,

a thousand knives struck through my back

and into my heart,

my heart loves far too easily,

gives in far too easily,

lets everyone in far too easily,

too quickly,

too soon,

too much.

my heart bleeds with every word,

my heart breaks with every breath,

every hug, every kiss,

my heart's fragile,

and it bleeds out like a cut artery,

it's damaged and bloody

but the blood is on my hands,

because no one else is willing

to take the blame

but me.

LOVELY HATRED

i hate you.

i hate you because i love you.

i hate you because you left, and

left me in the dust.

i hate you because you made me fall in love with you, then left

with no remorse.

i hate you because you kissed me hello,

then kissed me goodbye

i hate you for loving me,

choosing me,

for coming into my life, and making me feel like a blessing in disguise,

then leaving my side.

i hate you for giving me something worth losing,

i hate you

because

i love you.

FEARS AND PHOBIAS

growing up,

i feared so many things,

monsters, dinosaurs, supernatural beings,

i was a child amongst many others,

fearing what most feared,

but as i grew up i found something that i was more scared of,

something worth fearing

i realized losing something was scary,

scarier than anything before,

scarier than monsters, dinosaurs, or bloody mary.

i feared something real, something less extraordinary,

i feared losing you,

i feared

losing the only thing that made me happy.

WAITING

       i stay up nights waiting for
      a message from you, i spend hours
    staring at a blank white screen,
waiting for a
notification,
a sign to
know you
still love me.
   i wait,   i wait
    for your
      voice to
        bring me
          back to reality
            and help me breathe.

BLAH BLAH

i've lost what to say.

i'm at a loss for words.

i've forgotten how to speak—

blah, blah, blah,

i wonder other ways to say i love you

but the same thing comes out of my mouth,

and i forget everything my parents taught me,

i love you, but i can't just say *i love you*,

because i don't just

love you.

i cherish you,

i praise you,

but they all mean the same thing.

i love you.

but love is so hard to express because i could

hate you

but still love you because

i love you.

AIRPLANES

i like to look up at the stars when night comes, admiring the soft twinkle. i like to look up and wait for a shooting star.

i look up at the planes lighting up the sky, waiting for one to catch me, or for one to take you home.

I like to admire the natural beauty of the world, find peace in your absence, i like to stare at the clouds, wait for the rainfall, wait for the calming drops to collide with the windows.

i wait, and i look, i don't look away

'till my needs are at ease,

'till the rain comes,

and a star comes falling.

i look, and i wait, 'till one

of the planes carries

you in the midst of longing.

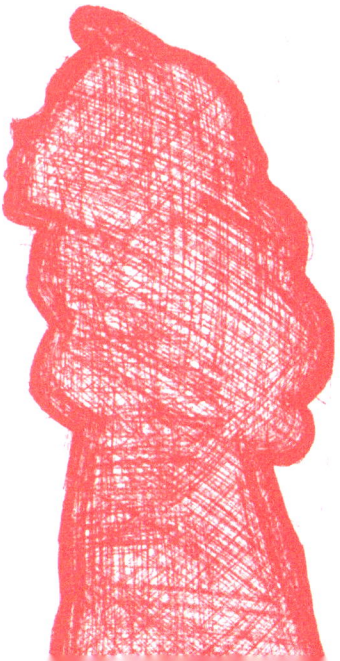

MINE

mine i thought when his lips passed the time,
mine i thought when he looked into my eyes

he was mine,
my dearest once-in-a-lifetime
i had found the one,
the holder of my heart,

mine i'd say
but then he left
without a second thought

HIM

i knew he was the one.

i knew he was the one when he didn't leave,

i knew he was the one when he told me he loved me.

i knew he was the one,

i knew he was the one the moment our eyes met.

the days pass and that feeling has stayed the same

he was the one for me

and i thought he always would be.

he was the one who makes me happy,

but he's no longer next to me.

i may never see him again

but he'll forever live in the back of my head

EMPTINESS

you've left me here with nothing

but my empty heart

and a soul longing for your touch.

DO YOU REMEMBER?

i remember when i first saw your face,

as your eyes laid upon me,

and i whispered out your name

under my breath, beneath the blazing stars,

the shooting and the falling,

a wish made silently.

i remember when you first spoke to me,

as your words threaded through my chest

like sunlight through stained glass.

i remember when you first touched me,

wrapped your hands around my waist,

pulled me in like ivy,

our vines intertwining.

i remember when you first kissed me,

pressed gently against my lips,

a soft and simple touch,

embedding a permanent place for your kiss

that couldn't be erased.

i remember when you first said *i love you*,

and the words flowed through me like water,

sinking into my skin,

melting into my bones giving a warmth

i didn't know i needed.

i remember when you left,

got over me,

said goodbye,

letting my whispers linger,

my stained glass dark,

my vines lonely,

a place missing on my lips,

and my bones cold,

missing the warmth i didn't know i needed.

COME

come to me, hold my hand through

chaos, love me in the dark and light, come

to me. choose me, my touch, and

take my hand.

ARE YOU STILL MINE?

i remember when we first kissed,

how i thought *you'd be mine*

but now i lay awake at night,

wondering if you think the same of someone else,

wondering if maybe it's really over,

if it's taken a turn for the worse.

wondering if you've found someone

that makes you light up and radiate with energy,

i'll never know what goes on in your world,

if you still love me.

will there be someone else who'll kiss and touch you the same way i used to?

is there someone on that bed that looks at you the same way i used to?

and the question keeps

running through my mind:

are you still mine?

MEMORIES

he lives in the back of my mind,

whispers lingering in my ear

his touch embedded into my skin,

his words of love engraved in my head.

i see him all the time,

i see him everyday but only in my mind

he lives in my head rent free

his hugs and kisses thriving

in my memory

every fight, mistake, *i love you's—*

i hate you's

running around my mind,

never seeming to die.

he lives inside of me,

as a boy i can't forget,

and he lurks inside my head.

PLAYER

my love was too heavy for you,

you couldn't hold on—

or perhaps you just didn't want to,

you had both hands open

but you kept throwing it back,

no energy to keep it up,

no time to hold it in your arms,

no love to keep together.

you played with my heart,

like a ball on a court,

you throw it against the ground,

player to player—

and in the hoop.

hate the player, not the game

but i can't bring myself

to hate you, regardless

how hard i try,

you'll always be the love

of my life,

in the back of my mind.

REMAINS

i'd lose it all,

risk everything,

if it meant keeping your memory,

i'd throw myself in the flames,

light myself on fire

if it meant your words would remain,

i'd tear myself to shreds,

stab my heart over and over again

if it meant having yours as my own.

i'd give everything—

i'd ruin all of me

if it meant having you in my remains,

i'd take my bones

and crush them to bits

if it meant tasting your kiss.

i'd surrender my whole body,

if it meant keeping your remains,

reminiscing of that time

we first met.

i'd lose it all,

risk everything,

if it meant your memory

would remain.

FRAGILE

love is so fragile—

my love was fragile.

a gust of wind and

the cradle goes down,

all hands on deck they'd shout,

but you can't flatten a crumpled paper

every word ran through my brain.

a never-ending cycle of hating and loving,

forgive and forget they'd say

but you can't put toothpaste back in it's bottle

they said i was fragile—sensitive,

let it roll of your shoulders!

but they didn't understand that

words can't be unsaid

my heart may have been glass,

fragile and delicate like a china plate,

throw it on the ground—

does it stay the same?

you can glue it back together,

repair it endlessly,

tape and tape,

paint and paint,

attempting to cover the cracks and stains

you can try to repair it,

but it'll never go back to the way it was,

it becomes more fragile,

more delicate,

more susceptible to breakage

my love was fragile,

but they were destructive,

and my heart couldn't be put back together.

MAYBE

maybe, in another life,

the stars would be brighter,

maybe, in another life,

you wouldn't seem as far,

maybe, in another life,

i could hold you in my arms

instead of saying *goodnight* to the stars

maybe,

just maybe,

i could be yours,

in some other world.

LOCKED HEART

take over my heart,

protect my heart,

make it yours

from dusk to

dawn, create

love through

blood.

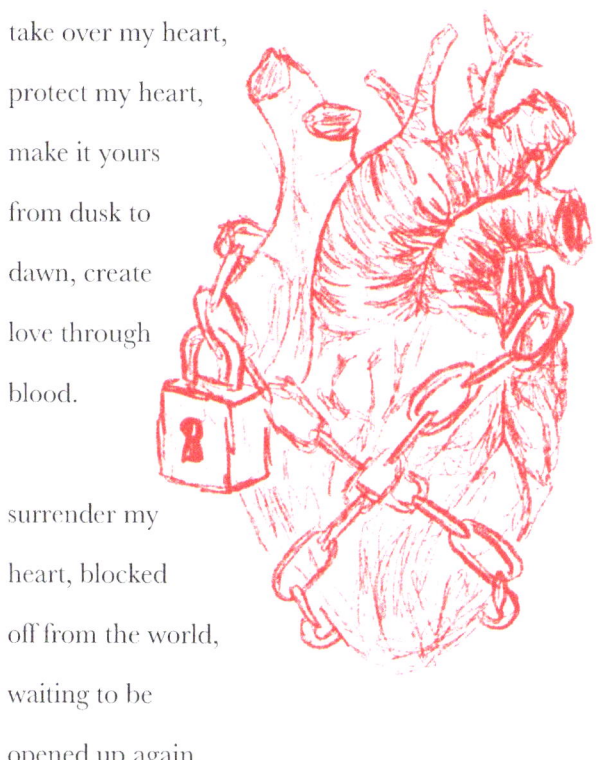

surrender my

heart, blocked

off from the world,

waiting to be

opened up again.

once you return.

BOYS

two years ago, i was sitting in an empty house at eleven p.m.

two years ago, i told a boy i wanted to die that didn't even care.

two years ago, i wrote a letter unlike this one,

one much darker, and horrid.

something that ended with *i'm sorry i couldn't do it.*

one year ago, i told a boy i was depressed.

one year ago, i told a boy i wanted to kill myself.

one year ago, i told a boy, and the boy loved me.

one year ago, a boy saved me

then one month ago, a boy left me

but then a week ago, a boy found me

at an end of a lunch table,

and chose me,

and didn't give up on me

regardless of what everyone else

had said,

regardless of the scars embedded in my skin,

one week ago, i told a boy i loved him,

one week ago, i found my one and only.

WORDS

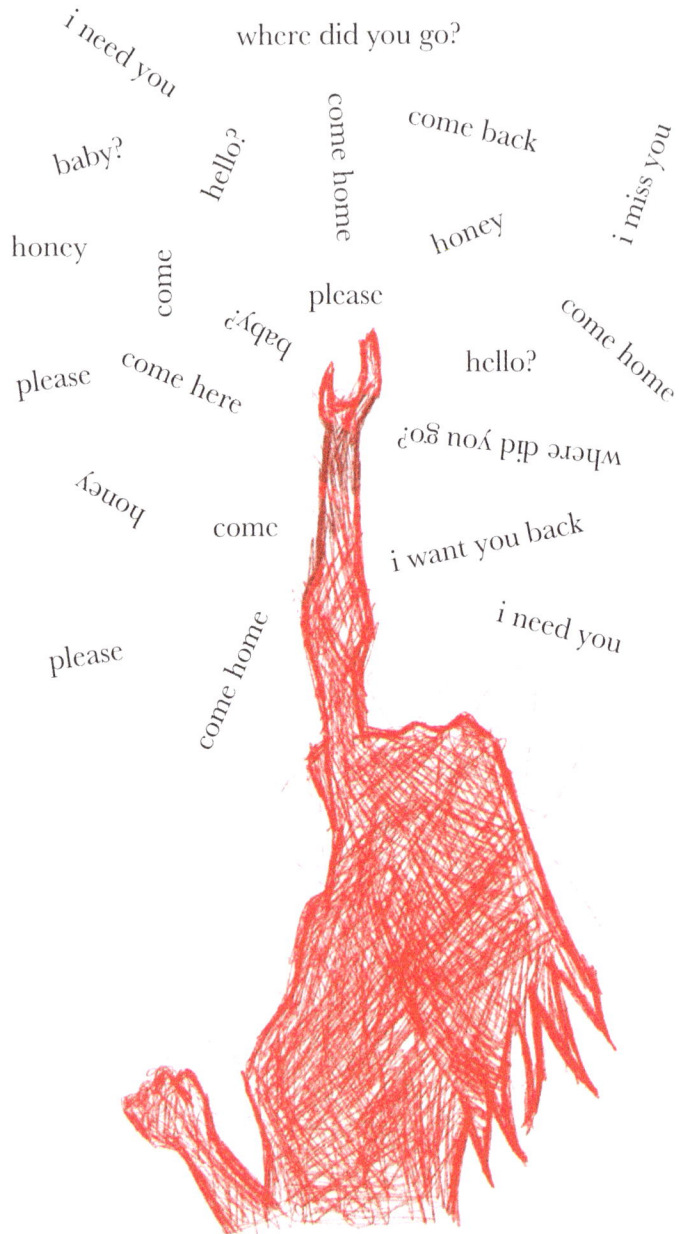

IF I WAS

if i was someone else,

someone named differently at birth,

someone with different colored hair,

and the hint of ocean blue in her eyes

would i still be the one?

if i looked any different,

would we still have fell in love?

if i acted the same but didn't go by that name,

would i still be yours?

or would i be like everyone else?

or would i still be your forever?

I STILL WANT YOU

without you i feel lost,

like i'm blind and can't see what's ahead,

my stick is broken, my hands are empty,

at any minute there could be an edge

without you everything hurts,

without your kisses to make it better.

how do i learn to live away from you?

how do you

teach a blind person to see

teach an animal to speak

teach a pig to fly

and teach time to wait?

the impossible can't be done.

you can't teach a heart not to break,

you can't teach me to live without you.

WISHES

i wish i could do it all over again

i wish i could go back to the day we first kissed

because that day my world got a little bit lighter,

my smile got a little bit brighter,

my life became a little bit clearer

i wish i was more forward.

i wish i would've just screamed *i love you*

instead of shying away.

i wish i would've said 'yes.'

i wish i was the girl that you had first met.

CLOUDS

is that you

i see in the clouds?

no, it's the vision of you i see

between every blink.

it's that gust of air that hisses your voice.

it's the thing i long for, what i want to see,

but it's not real.

no matter how much i want it to be.

TIMES

some days when we fight, it's like losing a part of myself.

sometimes, when i'm without you, i feel lost.

some nights, i can't sleep and feel like i'm screaming underwater waiting for you to show.

a lot of the time, i waste hours away just missing you, thinking about your sweet face.

a lot of the time, i'm writing your name in my math homework.

a lot of the time, i think of you.

and a lot of the time, i realize how much

i miss you

VISIONS OF YOU

when i lay in bed with the lights out,

your voice comes back to me

before everything goes quiet.

before my mind turns off,

i picture you next to me.

before everything,

the moment between night and day,

the moment where everything pauses,

where the world stops for a minute

it's as if you're right there next to me.

CANDLELIGHT

i had a spark,

i was a flame,

ignited — lit,

i kept it warm,

close to my heart,

where no one could blow it out.

i was a candlelight,

that lit up the night —

the life of the party,

everyone's best friend.

i was a fire,

but i made a mistake,

i gave my flame away,

for him to take,

perhaps he mistook me

for a birthday candle,

or a forest fire,

he blew out my flames,

and i was left

with the warmth of the smoke

i used all i had to reignite my flames,

even just a little,

it'll never be the same.

i managed to get a flame back,

a weak orange glow,

a small warm embrace,

but i made the same mistake

and gave him my flame

perhaps he mistook me for a match,

or a half melted candle,

he blew out the only flame i had,

and left me with nothing but

ash.

AUTHOR'S NOTE

I remember when I first started writing this book. My boyfriend had just moved to another country and long distance was a difficult process for me. I wanted to write about that, I wanted to capture the strong emotions that occur with long distance.

Halfway through the making of this book; we broke up. I was angry, heartbroken, disgusted and I felt betrayed.

I crossed out every poem about him I ever wrote, I ripped the papers to shreds in the same way he had destroyed my heart.

But as months went by, I kept coming back to this manuscript. I used to look at it full of anger but it slowly became a more bittersweet feeling.

At that time, I didn't just lose him, but I lost my best friend. I went from a high to an immediate low, and I didn't even know who I was anymore. Writing about him in a warm, worshipful light hurt me. On both the inside and out.

I procrastinated writing for months, because I was miserable. By then, I had found a new boy that I fell madly in love with very quickly.

But then he left too.

Now I am here, writing an author's note talking about all my heartbreaks that left me in the hospital.

I've never had good experiences with love. Not just with boyfriends but with friends, and crushes. I've always been a *second choice*, I've never been good enough.

It took a really long time for me to see my true worth, and realize that I didn't need romantic validation from someone to love myself. I began to hate the world, and treated everyone with hate because I never felt loved.

I decided I'm not writing this for a boy (or a girl.) I decided I'm not writing this for anyone, because at the end of the day, I write to get my feelings out. I write to make me happy, not just others.

I need to learn to love myself. I need to learn that my happiness is just as important as everyone else's.

I decided... I'm writing this one for *me*.

THE AUTHOR

Author photo © Makenzie Labani

MAKENZIE LABANI is a writer, artist, musician, and poet. She started writing at the age of thirteen, where she began writing her first published novel; '*Serenity.*' She has a dream of becoming a New York Times Bestseller while raising awareness on mental health and LGBTQ+ topics. She was born and raised in Houston, Texas. She's always been slightly different from the rest of her class, but that never stopped her from doing what she loves. She continues to pursue her passions while attending high school.

Made in the USA
Coppell, TX
03 February 2026

70983428R00069